All about Teeth

by Mari Schuh

Consulting Editor:
Gail Saunders-Smith, PhD

Consultant:
Lori Gagliardi CDA, RDA, RDH, EdD

Capstone press®

Mankato, Minnesota

Pebble Plus is published by Capstone Press,
1710 Roe Crest Drive, North Mankato, Minnesota 56003.
www.capstonepub.com

Library of Congress Cataloging-in-Publication Data
Schuh, Mari C., 1975–
   All about teeth/by Mari Schuh.
   p. cm. — (Pebble plus. Healthy teeth)
   Summary: "Simple text, photographs, and diagrams present information about teeth, including how to
take care of them properly" — Provided by publisher.
   Includes bibliographical references and index.
   ISBN: 978-1-4296-1238-8 (hardcover)
   ISBN: 978-1-4296-1784-0 (softcover)
   1. Teeth — Juvenile literature. I. Title. II. Series.
QP88.6.S38 2008
612.3'11 — dc22   2007027115

Editorial Credits
Sarah L. Schuette, editor; Veronica Bianchini; designer and illustrator

Photo Credits
Capstone Press/Karon Dubke, all

The author dedicates this book to her nephew, Alex Schuh of Tracy, Minnesota, who has 13 baby teeth.

Note to Parents and Teachers

The Healthy Teeth set supports national science standards related to personal health. This
book describes and illustrates the functions of teeth. The images support early readers
in understanding the text. The repetition of words and phrases helps early readers learn
new words. This book also introduces early readers to subject-specific vocabulary words,
which are defined in the Glossary section. Early readers may need assistance to read some
words and to use the Table of Contents, Glossary, Read More, Internet Sites, and Index
sections of the book.

Table of Contents

Teeth

Everyone's mouth
is full of teeth.
Lee started losing
his baby teeth
when he was 5 years old.

Permanent teeth grew
in the empty spaces.
Lee will have 32 permanent
teeth when he is an adult.

Parts of Teeth

Each of Lee's teeth
has its own size, shape,
and job.

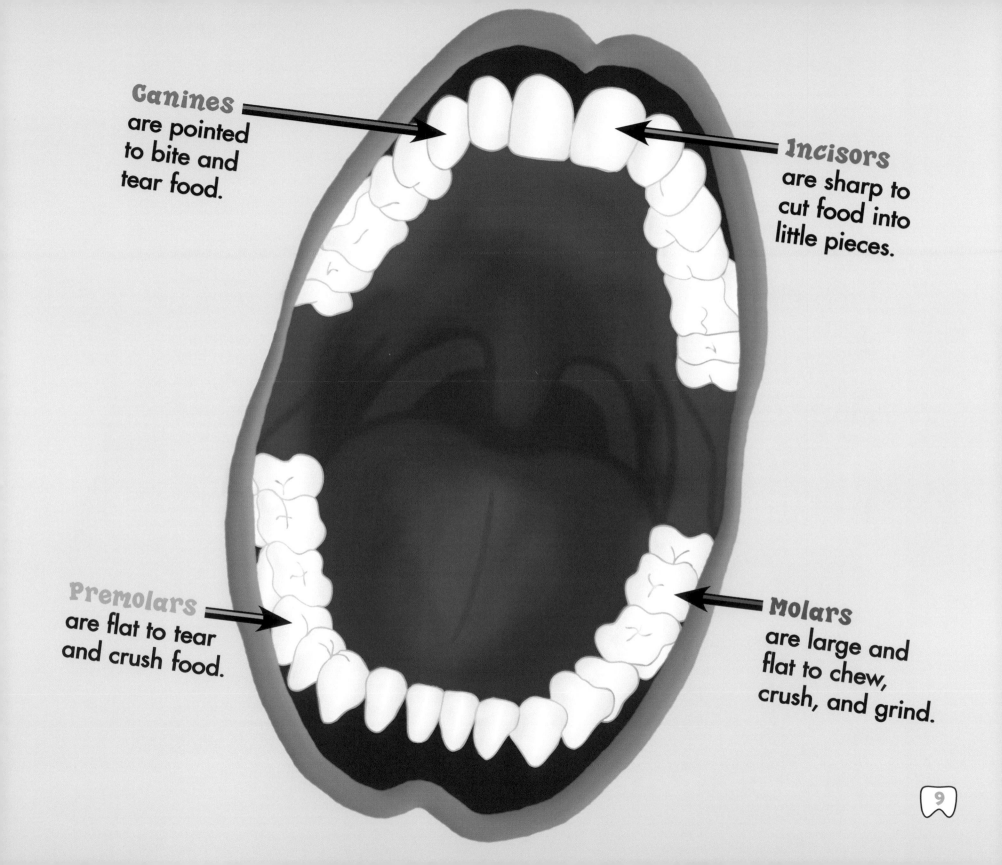

Canines are pointed to bite and tear food.

Incisors are sharp to cut food into little pieces.

Premolars are flat to tear and crush food.

Molars are large and flat to chew, crush, and grind.

9

Lee's sharp front teeth
bite and tear food.
His wide back teeth
mash food into small pieces.

The crown is the part
you can see.
Strong enamel covers
the crown.
Roots hold the teeth
into the gums.

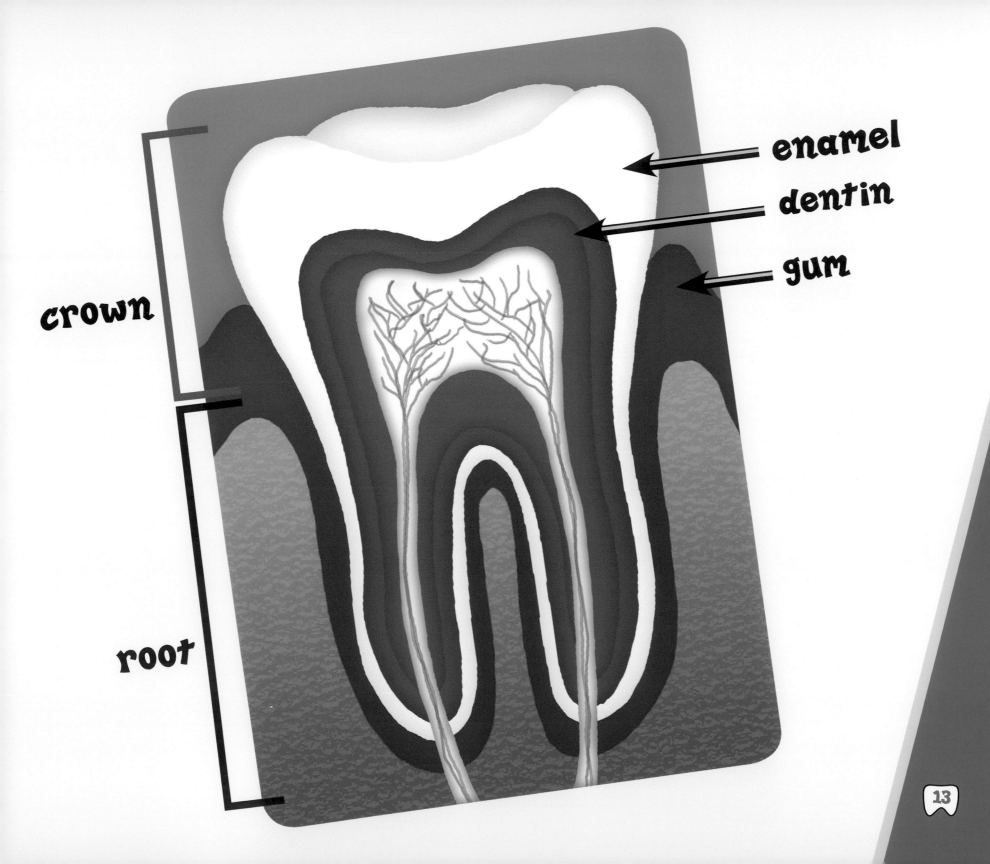

enamel

dentin

gum

crown

root

13

Healthy Teeth

Lee knows that eating
too many sweets
can give him cavities.
He brushes his teeth
at least twice every day.

Food gets stuck
between Lee's teeth.
He flosses every day
to keep his teeth
and gums healthy.

Lee visits the dentist's office
twice a year.
His teeth are cleaned
and checked for cavities.

Smile!

You should take care
of your teeth too.
You will have a healthy smile
your whole life!

Glossary

baby teeth — a child's first set of teeth; children have 20 baby teeth; baby teeth are also called primary teeth.

cavity — a decayed part or hole in a tooth

crown — the top part of a tooth that you can see

enamel — the hard, glossy covering on teeth; enamel protects teeth from decay.

gum — the firm skin around the base of teeth

permanent teeth — the teeth you have your whole life; most people have 32 permanent teeth.

root — the part of a tooth that holds it in the mouth; roots are found inside your gums.

Read More

Gaff, Jackie. *Why Must I Brush My Teeth?* Why Must I? North Mankato, Minn.: Cherrytree Books, 2005.

Llewellyn, Claire. *Your Teeth.* Look After Yourself. North Mankato, Minn.: Sea to Sea Publishing, 2007.

Royston, Angela. *Healthy Teeth.* Look After Yourself. Chicago: Heinemann, 2003.

Internet Sites

FactHound offers a safe, fun way to find Internet sites related to this book. All of the sites on FactHound have been researched by our staff.

Here's how:

1. Visit *www.facthound.com*

2. Choose your grade level.

3. Type in this book ID **142961238X** for age-appropriate sites. You may also browse subjects by clicking on letters, or by clicking on pictures and words.

4. Click on the **Fetch It** button.

FactHound will fetch the best sites for you!

Index

Word Count: 154
Grade: 1
Early-Intervention Level: 20